MW01675821

MANAGING FOR SUCCESS

Richard A. Jacobs, P.E.
Charles B. Dygert, Ph. D.

DEDICATION

To my father, Dick Jacobs and to Lew Gayner.
My mentors, who believed in me.
— Richard A. Jacobs

To "Captain" Ed Dygert, my father, and
Ken Dygert, my uncle. My leadership models.
— Charles B. Dygert

MANAGING FOR SUCCESS

ISBN: 1-884182-02-X

Published by Motivational Enterprises, Inc.
Box 28124
Columbus, OH 43228

Available at quantity discounts for bulk purchases.
For information, call 1-800-729-1293

Printed in the United States of America.

Contents

Foreword		5
Introduction		7
Chapter 1	*MORE THAN MANAGEMENT*	9
Chapter 2	*THE SYSTEMS APPROACH*	19
Chapter 3	*TAKE ME TO YOUR LEADER*	28
Chapter 4	*WHO HAS THE POWER?*	35
Chapter 5	*CULTURE, QUALITY AND STYLE*	44
Chapter 6	*HAIL TO THE CHIEF!*	52
Chapter 7	*THE PRESSURE TO PERFORM*	60
Chapter 8	*THE INTERACTIVE PARTNERSHIP*	70
Chapter 9	*WHO IS RESPONSIBLE?*	77
Chapter 10	*WHERE DO WE GO FROM HERE?*	86
References		94
About the Author		96

Foreword

In my travels as a speaker before educational and business groups in this country and abroad, it is clear that we are in the midst of a fundamental shift in the styles of management.

Thankfully, the era of autocratic, dictatorial leadership is coming to a close and being replaced by those who know what it means to be a coach, not a tyrant.

Today, managers are discovering what author Robert Fulgham learned in kindergarten: "Share everything. Play fair. Don't hit people."

In the book, *The Culture of Success*, which I co-authored with Richard A Jacobs, we presented a "how to" guide for transforming an organization into one guided by teamwork and a shared vision.

Now, in *Managing for Success,* we share with CEO's, managers and supervisors how they can *personally* apply these vital principles.

Those wanting to improve must be willing to address change. Do we compete internally, or do we cooperate? Do we recognize our human resources or do we take them for granted? Do we strive for excellence or do we settle for mediocrity?

We know that nothing happens overnight. Major shifts in the culture of nations and of organizations don't make sharp turns, they evolve. What does change quickly, however, are individuals who make the commitment to continual learning.

The message you are about to read will not only help you understand the change that is taking place, but will act as a blueprint for any current or future manager who desires to make more than a difference.

Parts of this book are written in the first person by Richard Jacobs, based on his personal experiences as a manager. We have collaborated on the basic premise that management is a *system* and how to integrate that system into a quality culture. The management and business approaches described are philosophically consistent with mine and integrate well the Deming principles that form the heart of the message I share with my audiences each year.

— *Charles B. Dygert, Ph.D.*

Introduction

Victor Hugo once said, "Nothing is more powerful than an idea whose time has come."

Today, after being involved in business and management for more than four decades, I am convinced that management is a state of mind. It is a philosophy, an attitude, an *idea.*

After years of hearing about the "systems" approach to management, it suddenly struck me like a thunderbolt that *management itself is a system.* It is that simple, but powerful concept that is the core of this book.

This system has six inter-related components: *Leadership, Power, Culture, Accountability, Interactivity* and *Responsibility.*

In this information-driven, global, dynamic economy, transformation is taking place almost faster than many organizations can handle it. Everything is in flux — new technology, distributions systems and consumer demands.

When you discover how certain components of an organization are inter-related, your entire view of managing and decision making will be altered.

To guide an organization toward a quality culture involves the ability to rethink traditional management styles and move to an environment of democratic participation by everyone in the organization. As a manager, you have the opportunity to produce this environment.

On these pages you'll learn:

- How to develop your philosophy of management.
- How to identify the levels of management.
- The consequences of your management style.
- How to understand the "zone of effectiveness."
- Managing through the six "inter-related components."
- Proven strategies for leadership.
- The nature of power.
- How to build a quality culture.
- How to achieve through the dynamics of interactivity.
- How to develop core competencies.
- How to prepare for the future.

Let me encourage you to not only read these words, but to make them come alive. I believe *managing for success* is more than an objective, it must become a way of life.

1

More than Management

Anyone can be a manager. It's a profession with virtually no entry barriers.

To become a nurse, a certified public accountant, a professional engineer, a doctor or a lawyer requires specific formal training and testing.

Yes, there are some organizations that have set minimum qualifications, but in the vast majority of cases management is an equal opportunity for all.

Opportunity, however, does not guarantee achievement. During my years of corporate management I have met countless individuals who have learned a great deal *about* supervision and administration, yet they did not produce positive results.

If you are looking for a manual about management as an occupation or a career, this it not it. This book is concerned with only one objective — managing for *success.*

As you will soon discover, the tools of a successful manager are not clever formulas or simple platitudes. Instead they are a philosophy, an attitude, an approach that is part of a system that will serve you for a lifetime.

What's Your Philosophy?

How much time have you given to developing a personal management philosophy? Has it been formulated clearly? Can you articulate it? Can you teach it to someone else?

A management outlook will determine how you approach situations and implement leadership. It may be based on observations, practical experience, extensive reading or examples from a mentor or teacher.

My personal view is based on the extensive input of two mentors: my father, Richard A. Jacobs (a career executive with Brockway Glass) and Lewis F. Gayner — the person I reported to during most of my fifteen years after graduate school.

My mentors spent a great deal of time indoctrinating me with managerial training, process knowledge, company economics, strategic planning, and culture. They also led by example, particularly in working with people..

In addition to the trials and errors of corporate life, I have also been greatly influenced by the writings of Douglas McGregor of MIT, Douglas Brown of Princeton, and A. H. Maslow of Brandeis — all college professors who wrote in the 1950s and 60s about the human side of organizations.

The sources I have identified as the basis for my view of business are closely aligned with the field of psychology — an understanding that is vital in working with a wide variety of personalities.

Briefly let me share my philosophy; not only to give you insight into my methods of operation, but to help you reflect on your own conclusions.

I feel that the cornerstone of one's management philosophy is the answer to this question: "What do I truly believe about people?"

The noted psychologist A. H. Maslow states: "The person who tends to believe that all people are essentially good will show the same resistance to change of this belief as will the person who believes all people are essentially bad."[1]

My two mentors focused on the "good" and so do I.

1. People Policy.

- Be concerned with people as people — not with who is right.
- Don't just create a team, join it!
- The attitude and behavior of people on the job is based primarily on their own work experiences.
- Each person must assume the responsibility for accomplishment — to himself, his company, and the company's customers.
- Develop an attitude of not just doing what we like to do but learning to like what we have to do.

- Morale is a capital asset worth as much as a good product, a good location, or money in the bank. It cannot be purchased; it must be deserved!

2. Labor and Management

- Workers want to be part of something worthwhile.
- Pride of achievement or creation produces the strongest satisfaction.
- Workers must be both paid and recognized for their accomplishments. They expect to be compensated in accordance with their achievements and feel a measure of security in their jobs.
- Workers want to work for leaders whom they can respect. Leaders must earn respect, be democratic in their dealings and be competent in their chosen fields.
- Employees want a chance to progress and should be informed when opportunities exist.
- Employees want a chance to participate in management training and in decisions which concern them.
- People deserve to work in congenial surroundings.

3. Communication

- To communicate effectively, you must practice the art of listening.
- Management should establish an open door policy and communicate with employees on a first name basis.
- Exhibit respect for all people in the organization.

- Get to know families, not just employees.
- Solicit the opinions of others.
- Always greet people "eye to eye."
- Correct people as needed; analyze with them regarding how to improve..
- Conduct periodic one on one discussions to review performance, problems and goals.
- Managers must have the visibility and knowledge to establish policies and priorities using input from peers and subordinates, as well as the person they report to.
- Keep your ego in check and avoid arrogance.
- Practice patience —but not unlimited patience.
- Discuss performance, goals, and problems on a "formal basis" at least twice a year.

4. Work Ethic

- You must be responsible and accountable for your job, earn your own way, and make a contribution to the company.
- Constantly seek help and cooperation.
- Strive for excellence in all you do.
- Honestly face work problems. Ask, "Is the trouble with the job or with me?"
- Be ready to work long hours but also work "smart."
- Learn to trust others and delegate.
- Set a good example.
- Have "fun" at work and at home.
- Strive for a high quality of life.

5. Performance — Good Judgment

- Good judgment is a combination of knowledge and the capacity to use it subjectively.
- Every executive must reserve the right to determine the priorities of attention and action.
- Success is related to proper selection of issues needing attention and choosing the right time for action.
- The best system cannot substitute for good people.
- Improve the quality of management personnel at every level.
- Constantly "raise the bar" or standard — which is only possible if internal cooperation replaces internal competition.
- Welcome external competition to produce your best.

6. Values

- Every manager must first be something and *believe* in something before he can influence others.
- Believe in yourself.
- Practice good ethics and set an example of what is right.

7. Time Management

- Don't waste your own time or the time of others.
- Meetings should be well run, to the point and informal.

8. Leadership

- Personal characteristics critical to leadership are:
  Intelligence: to think through complex issues.
  Stability: inner poise creating consistency of action.
  Empathy: put yourself in the other person's place.
  Social sensitivity: understanding people as a group.
  Moral courage: conviction to take the right course of action and the blame for failure when appropriate.
  Resilience: ability to bounce back after failure.

- The higher you rise in management, the more dependent you are on accurate information.
- Maintain a vision of the future.

9. Business Knowledge

- Learn and master the economics of your business.
- Learn the internal processes and what drives your market.
- Become a systems thinker; expand your knowledge of "people" systems.

10. Customers

- "Good enough" is not enough! Strive to do a better job, make a better product, give better quality and value. Failure is not an option.

- Quality is your best sales tool.
- The customer and the company are on the same team. Both need each other.
- Act on problems immediately.
- Invite customers to visit you — and visit them *often.* Encourage a partnership relationship.

11. Culture

- Understand that your approach to people is as important as methods, standards and procedures.
- "Turf building" must never be encouraged — it only builds walls..
- Build a positive team chemistry so that everyone functions effectively.
- Create a total environment for success.

12. Management Style

- Be enthusiastic about getting to work and making things happen.
- Develop an informal "walk around" management style.
- Exhibit strong, positive feelings about the company. Buy stock in it. Show "ownership."
- Speak up on issues without trying to be "politically correct."
- Encourage input from others before making a decision, but retain accountability. People are often not acclimated to working in a cooperative

environment with shared decision making. They will need to be taught.

- Be a consistent, but not a *patterned* manager (with a predictable daily routine).
- Work to stay self-motivated to deal with day to day problems; but also develop skills to deal with a crisis.
- Don't become so involved in the day to day details that you lose the focus on the big picture.
- Recognize and give credit for good ideas.

The Vital Ingredients

Since the art or practice of managing is constantly evolving, the development of your philosophy will also be changing. However, you will eventually be guided by a set of heartfelt beliefs and core convictions that will anchor your future.

Ron Read, Director of Process Development for ITT Cannon believes we need a set of essential content skills to be effective leaders and managers that "center on our abilities to motivate our teams, use effective management styles and communicate with subordinates, peers, and supervisors."[2]

Specifically, Read recommends that managers have a grasp of the Motivation Needs Hierarchy based on the work of Maslow and Herzberg and an understanding of the Management Grid and Theory X and Y styles of management by Douglas McGregor.

If you've read *The Culture of Success*, the book I co-authored with Dr. Charles Dygert, you know how committed I am to building a working environment of cooperation where everyone is intrinsically concerned — where another's success brings feelings of personal accomplishment.

Just as a quality culture is a workplace with an "attitude," it should also be your approach to management.

I have come to the conclusion that attitude is more important than facts, history, education, money, circumstances, failures, successes, appearances, talent, skill, or what other people think, say or do.

It will make or break an organization, a church, or a home. The remarkable thing is that we have a choice every day regarding the outlook we will embrace.

We cannot change the inevitable, but we certainly can play on the one string we have — our attitude. As author Charles Swindoll states, "I am convinced that life is 10% what happens to me and 90% how I react to it."

It's *you*, not your title, position or power that is vital. As Douglas McGregor of M.I.T. stated: "Management cannot provide a man with self-respect, or with the respect of his fellows, or with the satisfaction of needs for self-fulfillment. It can create conditions such that he is encouraged and enable to seek such satisfactions for himself and it can thwart him by failing to create these conditions."[3]

The key to success is in your hand.

2

The Systems Approach

The role of a manager is drastically changing. The days are gone when a person was hired to oversee a group of employees who were focused on a narrow isolated task.

Today, that same person is involved in issues that affect nearly everyone in a corporation or organization.

What is meant by management?

- Management is leading ordinary people to do extraordinary things.
- Management is the psychology of understanding how to get people to cooperate.

- Management is the mind set of accepting responsibility for your work and the work of others.
- Management is believing that a quality culture can produce excellence.
- Management is a process.
- *Management is a system.*

Up the Ladder

Like the game of baseball, management can be played on several levels. The higher the plateau, the more difficult and complex the assignment and the responsibility.

Here are the three basic levels:

Level I — Supervisor

The introductory, or "supervisory" level is responsible for a single department. Usually, this person is the interface between the management of the organization and the workers — both clerical and manual.

Supervisors are involved in daily work assignments, productivity, quality, planning and interpersonal problems within their designated area.

Level II — Manager

At this level — often a site or plant manager — the responsibility for a major unit of the enterprise rests with this individual. He or she reports to the larger organization.

The manager directs supervisors to carry out functions within the plant or office and provides the interface or link between that facility and the rest of the organization. They are responsible for maintaining a highly motivated work force and creating a quality working environment.

Level II managers have the advantage of being able to exert great influence since they have direct contact with the levels above and below. This is illustrated in the Zone of Effectiveness.

Zone of Effectiveness

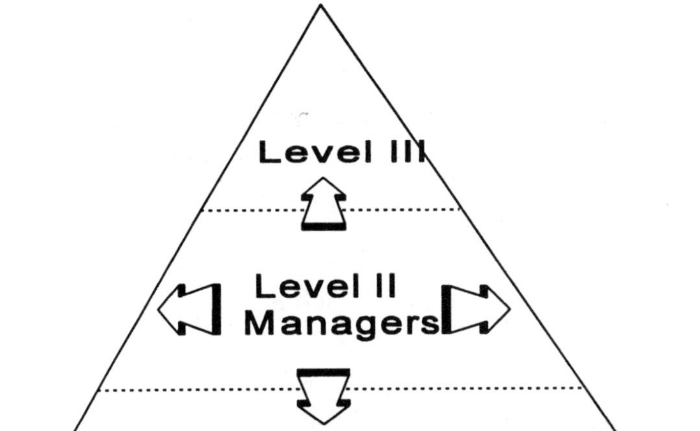

Level III — Executive

It is here that the strategic direction of the organization (and the securing of resources to make it happen) takes place. Leadership and vision are a *must*.

The executive becomes the link between the Board of Directors — who must approve the direction of the enterprise — and management.

As an individual moves upward through the management levels, each promotion brings a great deal more complexity into play — involving people, technology, markets, competitors, shareholders, regulators, legislators, and other factors.

While there are many variations of these three levels, and they may be called by other names, their functions are basic to almost every business or organization.

The Six Components

Managing is a dynamic and evolving process composed of six inter-related components.

1. **Leadership** — providing vision, values, direction, strategy and encouragement.
2. **Power** — centers of influence that determine what happens internally; source of authority.
3. **Culture** — the mores, habits, and "the way we do things" in an organization.

4. **Accountability** — measuring performance and being answerable for "the bottom line."
5. **Interactivity** — the communication, cooperation and competition found within the culture.
6. **Responsibility** — accepting the task of solving problems, making decisions and completing the work.

Unless managers utilize all the components at their disposal they become like a car that is not running on all cylinders.

Management is a System
With Six Inter-related Components Each Having Many Subparts

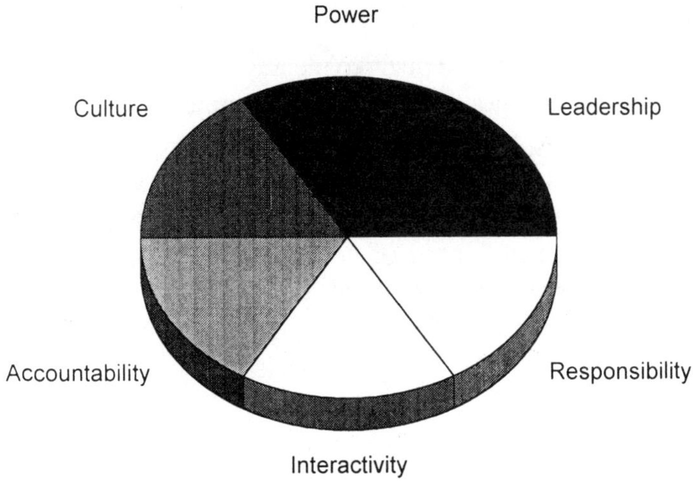

Why is an understanding of the levels and components of management necessary? Systems thinking requires both a knowledge of the parts and an understanding of the relationship between the parts and the "whole."

How it Works

Today's business leaders are faced with a world that is increasingly more complex. By embracing a systems approach to management — and understanding that management *itself* is a system — the relationships that cause the complexity can be broken down so that better decisions can be more easily made.

The systems approach is not some deep, mysterious process grasped only after sitting on a mountain top for hours in deep contemplation. No. It is really quite simple. By charting the processes currently used in your organization, you will begin to identify the systems and the relationships among the various departments.

You might begin by tracing the process of product development, then chart the flow among the organization's functional centers. It is important not only to "chart the flow" but to take note of both subjective and objective performance measures. What is the attitude of management and workers? What does the data about productivity and quality say? Who are the decision makers? Each of these factors should be noted.

There are literally hundreds of concepts you can factor

into the process. Finally, you will no longer be seeing the parts, but the whole. You will have a "feel" for the organization and will begin to manage from an entirely new perspective.

The reason systems thinking is often difficult is because we have been taught to think in "air tight compartments" of either-or, black-white and cause-effect.

As one of my colleagues put it, "The scientific method may be great for science, but it certainly is not the way we ought to see an organization."

How can this approach be defined? Peter Senge, author of *The Fifth Discipline,* says, "At its broadest level, systems thinking encompasses a large and fairly amorphous body of methods, tools, and principles, all oriented to looking at the interrelatedness of forces, and seeing them as part of a common process."[1]

It has been refreshing to see engineers sit down with psychologists and public relations executives confer with custodians to work on company problems.

The solution to problems can usually be solved by your own people if you just solicit their opinions and advice.

The Connection

The systems approach requires both an understanding of the process and the relationships among its parts. Knowing and having a belief in methods, standards and procedures will provide knowledge of the process. Understanding human behavior and our approach to people will help explain the relationships. Unless you embrace both — and are willing to remain on a course of continual learning — your chances of becoming a systems thinker are limited.

In his insightful book, *The Democratic Corporation*, Russell L. Ackoff makes the point that no part of a system has an independent effect on the system of which it is a part. As an example, he states that "the way the heart affects the body depends on what the lungs are doing, and the way the lungs affect the body depend on what the heart, brain, and other parts are doing."[2]

Applied to business, Ackoff says, "The way a manufacturing department affects a corporation's performance depends on the behavior of its marketing department."

When you begin to think in terms of systems those relationships begin to come alive. And it's a study that never ends.

Peter V. Vaill, in his important book, *Learning as a Way of Being*, writes, "Systems thinking immerses the thinker in a process of ongoing inquiry." Says Vaill, it is therefore "continual learning. Because of the very nature of systems, it cannot be anything else."[3]

Within an organization there are "ways" we do things which form the basis for the systems that allow it to function.

To change an organization and get it on the road to continuous improvement requires the understanding of the managing process and a critical review of how each function is related.

In managing change it is much more effective to find out what is wrong with the system(s) rather than focusing on personalities or people.

In most cases, by correcting the process, people are able to become productive. With this approach we are blaming "what" but not "who."

For years we have been told why managers need to become "systems thinkers." On this journey we may have overlooked an even more powerful fact — that *management itself is a system.*

3

Take Me to Your Leader

From my earliest days in business I have heard people debate this question: "Are leaders *born* or are they *made?"*

As a result of working with a great variety of executives over several decades, I am convinced that leadership is a state of mind — a learned response — that eventually becomes a person's managerial style. At the same time, inside that person must be some "native ability" which rises to the occasion.

We hear much about the importance of *charisma,* but the necessary ingredient is *confidence* — both *in* the leader and *by* the leader.

Here is another question to ponder: "Do leaders rise to

the top in a crisis or is it the crisis that develops the leader?"

I believe emergency situations simply reveal whether or not a person has what it takes to be in charge.

How does an individual know if he or she has the qualities to lead? An instant barometer is the surge of adrenalin and feeling of exhilaration that accompanies the opportunity.

On the other hand, the person who reacts with fear, anxiety and helplessness is not the right one for the mission.

Checking on the Troops

When a company's leadership is autocratic, the system of operation is usually bureaucratic. The two are twins.

In those organizations, valuable time is wasted on an archaic approval process when the focus should be on removing barriers. Workers and supervisors are constantly waiting for someone to act or give approval. And what is top management doing? They are usually checking on those below because the bridge of mutual trust has not been built.

Without effective leadership an organization is simply reacting to events.

When that happens, the internal in-fighting escalates and a form of anarchy eventually takes over.

In a quality culture, however, leadership and vision spirals down from top management and captures the imagination of employees at every level. It is a total participative process — not only in words, but in action.

When managers stop being watch-dogs and begin listening to employees there will be a marked improvement in the health of the organization.

How can we know that leadership is effective? Two things will happen:

1. Followers, subordinates and peers of the leader stop being personally worried or pre-occupied with their own fate.
2. Employees put their faith in the leader's ability to represent their best interests and find the solution to the organization's survival and success.

Effective managers consistently discuss concerns with their "troops," then develop plans they put into action — ready to defend them at all costs.

One Agenda

It is difficult for employees to know how to become leaders when they have spent their entire careers being told what to do — or waiting for orders.

What is the point of giving someone authority when it simply means carrying out actions dictated to them from the top?

That's why a new model — a systems approach — is essential.

To test the concept that *management is a system,* observe what happens when the leadership is changed. There is a direct impact on the other components (power, culture, accountability, interactivity and responsibility) of the system. If someone in leadership is removed and there are no changes when the new person assumes the position, then your "system is broken" and you have not truly appointed a leader.

The transformation to a quality culture won't happen by accident. Managers at all levels must create an environment of internal cooperation and constantly share the dream for the organization's future. They can't stop until the vision of excellence becomes the heartbeat of the entire workforce.

Tsun-Yan Hsieh, director at the Toronto, Canada, offices of McKinsey & Company, states that "A vision is a vivid picture of what an organization wants to be. Visions, in part, must be rational. Visions must be strategically sound and logically compelling so that the people understand precisely what changes in performance and organizational behavior will be necessary to achieve it. Visions that evoke extraordinary performance have three things in common: a noble purpose, a sense of urgency, and clear boundaries."[1]

How do you get everyone on the "same page?"

You start by making sure each team member has an understanding of the past — key events, people, and performance that brings the enterprise to it's present moment. When that is fully understood, you are ready to tackle the future.

Since people enter the organization at different points of time, everyone's experience is unique — and so is their perception of the enterprise.

Every person craves the answer to these two questions:

What is the future of the organization?
What is my future in the organization?

Successful leaders never hesitate to address these issues.

Filling the Void

The person who has been handed the reigns of leadership can never shy away from responsibility. The slightest retreat results in a lack of trust and it will be difficult to regain the status once enjoyed.

Unfortunately, that is what has happened to many in government, education and in corporate America. The "trickle down" theory is not only about money, it's about leadership. When it declines at the top, it affects everything beneath.

Everywhere, we need people who will stand up, take charge and accept accountability — not for personal recognition, greed or power, but for the sole purpose of improving the condition of the company, the institution or the nation.

The code of ethics that guides the organization must be more than a written statement; it must be personal.

Jack Welch, CEO of General Electric, said, "The only way I know to create trust is by laying out your values and then walking the talk."[2]

How do we fill the leadership void? We can start by identifying those who manage only for a paycheck, a lofty title or the prestige. They must be replaced by those who believe that a strong organization is the result of vision, commitment, teamwork, integrity and purpose.

Warren Bennis and Burt Nanus, in their excellent book, *Leaders: The Strategies for Taking Charge*, write, "People talk about the decline of the work ethic. But what there really is, is a *commitment gap*. Leaders have failed to instill vision, meaning, and trust in their followers. They have failed to empower them. Regardless of the type of organization, the key and pivotal factor needed to enhance human resources is leadership."[3]

I believe the most important decision an executive in business can make today is to be courageous and make the *right* decision — not the "politically correct" one.

Remember, management is a system and it is leadership that sets the tone.

4

Who Has the Power?

The neglected component in most management systems can be stated in one word: *Power!*

It's always there, but people don't like to talk about it. Perhaps that is because the word itself causes people to think about "command and control" leadership where workers are in subjection to a taskmaster.

Power may be positive, negative, or neutral, yet it is constantly present.

- It may not provide leadership but it retains veto rights.
- It determines how resources will be allocated.
- It approves who will be in the key positions.

- It significantly influences customers and suppliers.

What every member of an organization must realize, however, is that power — the *right* kind — is necessary for fulfilling the mission.

Where does power come from? There are two diametrically opposing views — both of which are partially correct.

Theory number one: Power originates from the top — from those with authority.
Theory number two: Power rises from the people who are being directed — who will give it up freely when they feel it is in their best interest.

Often, the person placed in charge of an organization may have both authority and accountability but *no power.* If this is the case, people will sense it and seek to align themselves with what — or *who* — they perceive to be the dominant force.

Win-Win

If you were to ask the employees of a typical company, "Who has the power?" they would instantly turn to theory number one. They would tell you how it rests at the top of the hierarchy pyramid. You might even hear detailed explanations such as: "The shareholders have entrusted the Board of Directors with their interests and empowered them to develop a slate of officers for their approval. Management is then entrusted with the authority to get the job done."

Most workers fail to realize that management can't reach it's goals without the cooperation of the entire work force.

Who has the *real* power? The employees. Why? Because they have the ability to cooperate or to withhold cooperation.

Do you see why creating an environment of unity and teamwork is essential? It unleashes the collective intellect and produces almost limitless power.

When both management and employees conclude that it is mutually advantageous to work together, a quality culture begins to emerge. It becomes a win-win situation.

Getting Results

Often, the question is not who *has* the power, but who *wants* the power.

With a position of control comes prestige — and that can stroke many egos. Unfortunately, far too many executive decisions are based on the desire to retain power. Often it becomes an obsession that sets the agenda for the entire organization.

Let's pose the question another way: Who *needs* the power?

I believe a manager should have enough power — in the form of authority — to obtain results within his or her span of control.

An appreciation for the impact of authority is key to understanding how the managerial process works.

"Naive" is the only word I can think of to describe the working knowledge of many managers on this topic.

Power skills must be in the managers toolbox. As stated by Dr. John P. Kotter, professor of organizational behavior at Harvard Business School, "Managers who have little skill at or inclination toward power-oriented behavior sometimes remain in low-level managerial jobs throughout their careers, with few subordinates and few coordination responsibilities."[1]

On the other hand, Kotter believes that people who have power-oriented tendencies and proficiencies are usually successful in managerial careers, "Because job dependence tends to increase with the level of hierarchy.

The greater a person's power skills and inclinations, the further he or she rises in that hierarchy (all other factors being equal)."

Knowledge is Power

A major shift is taking place as we enter the 21st century. Today, the information superhighway is delivering vast amounts of facts and data at an unprecedented pace. In the past this information has been available only to a select few — and many leaders hoarded their storehouse of knowledge because it gave them tremendous leverage over the work force.

Now, that same data is being accessed by anyone with a curiosity and a computer modem. As a result we have employees who are extremely well-informed and who will no longer tolerate the practices of the past.

Forces in Conflict

When managers attempt to change an organization and those who control the resources are determined to retain the status quo, the battle lines are drawn. It is a classic confrontation between the *retention of power* and the *exercise of leadership*.

The executive is striving to "reach out," take risks, and move the organization to new heights, while the "power monger's" objective is to retain or increase their base of authority. In other words, the leader is introducing change while the power broker is entrenched in the status quo.

How can the impasse be broken? The "vision" must become the single agenda in an organization and be accepted by all of the stakeholders.

As the following illustration expresses, influence starts at the top of the leadership pyramid and spreads downward.

The Zone of Influence

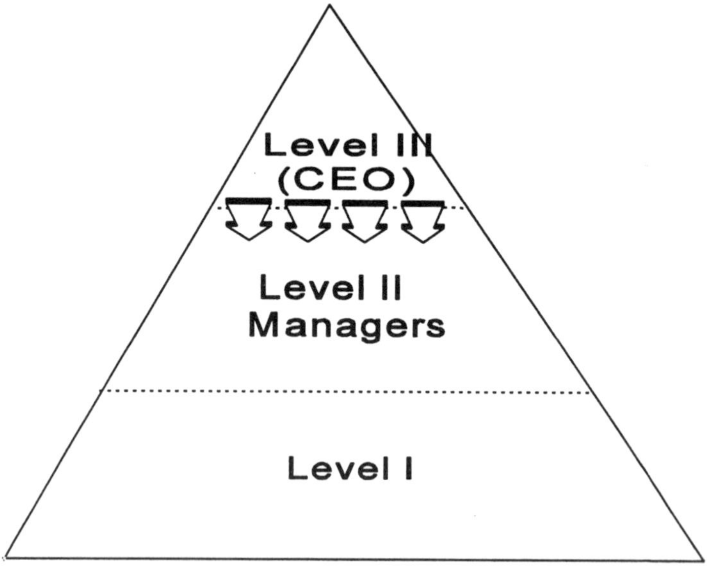

The Exercise of Authority

Here's the phrase that symbolizes an autocratic,

traditional culture of bureaucratic management: "Who gave you the authority to do that?"

It is the blanket under which unsure, unsteady, non-confident people hide and is a signal to instill fear and make threats. Another version is: "Who told you to do that?" Nothing kills initiative more quickly than confronting someone with those words.

When managers exercise undue authority over others it results in a workforce becoming obsessed with "getting even." Does that provide for a productive work environment? Hardly.

Empowerment — or Endullment?

When you give authority to a person or a team to enable them to move toward their goal without having to seek approval each step of the way, you have suddenly *empowered* them.

The power we are talking about may be temporary or permanent. Short-term authority has been called, "power on a string" since it can be pulled back or withheld at any time.

The term <u>empowerment</u> implies scope, yet it is rarely all-encompassing. Boundaries must always be established before the work begins.

The opposite of empowerment has been called *endullment*. According to Dr. John Dew, manager of strategic planning at Lockheed Martin Utility Services, "Endullment is the dulling of people's minds as a result of nonparticipation. It occurs in schools and it happens at work. Endullment leads to low motivation, poor attendance, refusal to cooperate to improve the system, and defeatism. It conditions people to be apathetic about the world around them."[2]

Shifting Gears

Empowerment is an example of a *power sharing* within an organization. It impacts not only the "distribution of power," but other components — and is directly related to leadership since it comes from the top.

The system dynamics of *leadership* and *power* have been widely discussed since the linkage of these two forces creates the culture and affects the *who, what, when* and *how* parts of accountability, interactivity and responsibility.

These shifts in leadership and power are constantly evolving as people retire, resign, are promoted, come into an organization, etc. Every manager in the system must have an awareness of this phenomenon and avoid working in what has been called a *cave* – or *"bunker"– mentality.*

Our personal progress depends on:

- Understanding the dynamics of the management system.

- Becoming willing to make continual improvements.
- Fitting into the culture.
- Sharing the values of the organization.

The Greatest Power

We have been given the opportunity to exercise influence and steer the direction of the enterprise. However, we must never forget that the greatest power resides in our employees and our customers. As many managers learn too late, the ultimate decisions rest with them.

What's the bottom line? If you want to produce results, tap into the power that derives from an environment of teamwork and unity.

5

Culture, Quality and Style

What is culture? It is simply the working environment and "the way we do things." It is greatly influenced, however, by management styles, systems, beliefs, behavior, habits and values shared by members of the organization.

Moving to a *quality* culture requires transformation.

According to Dr. W. Edwards Deming, American industry either has to change or face a challenge to its survival. He referred to this as a transformation that must be initiated by management.

In many environments, change can be traumatic and may be actively resisted. Neil H. Snyder, co-author of

Vision, Values and Courage, observes: "This is why the role of the leader in developing a quality culture is so critical. Only strong leadership communicating a shared vision can guide an organization through the change needed for a quality orientation. Without the vision and commitment of top management, achieving quality results will remain an illusive dream."[1]

A New Vantage Point

The journey to a quality culture requires new thinking in the way people in the organization perceive the world and their roles in it. They must:

- Be willing to become involved in restructuring and reengineering.
- Embrace computer technology as an ally, not an adversary.
- Recognize constantly changing demands for products and services.
- Think regional, national and global.
- Management must communicate a shared vision with the people.

Managers must articulate the mission and the need for innovation without becoming defensive or overly fanatical. They must stay the course!

How long does it take to shift to the new leadership style? From my experience and observations it takes from three to seven years — depending on how deeply ingrained the old systems exist in the workplace and whether top management has to be replaced more than once.

Success in this effort is measured by (1) the dedication and commitment to change, (2) consistency of training in the new arena, and (3) how well the rationale for change is communicated to the people.

Human behavior shifts will not occur until individuals — at all levels of the enterprise — receive proper training on the emerging behavior patterns necessary to accommodate the new team environments.

Management Style

Over time, every manager develops a unique personal style that is formed by his or her management philosophy, personality or behavior type and the surrounding organizational culture. In addition, it will be influenced by the unique qualities of the region or nation.

A manager with "no style" is like a chameleon — changing with the surroundings. The person may survive as an employee but will gain little respect as a manager.

Different strokes produce different folks. Autocratic

types of leadership stimulate internal *competition,* while democratic modes spur internal *cooperation.*

Therefore, the transformation of an organization's culture is based on the success of the leadership moving the *management system* methodically toward a democratic model based on team methods

Where's the Action?

Most managers can be labeled as either *action* or *non-action* managers. Those in the "action" group can be described as being in one (or more) of four broad categories:

Category 1: Leaders — those who create the vision, give direction, develop a positive work environment and expect and achieve beneficial results.

Category 2: Managers — those who can lead people and manage things to achieve high performance — measured by both productivity and quality. These individuals are organized and "driven" for results.

Category 3: "Strawbosses" — this is a rather old, but descriptive name for first level supervisors who both give direction and do the work.

Category 4: Tyrants/Dictators — this is the "boss" who is in charge and wants everyone to know it. The personality may be kindly or "impossible," abrasive or benevolent, but stays in a *command and control* mode.

When we want managers to develop into "the total

package" we are looking for a combination of categories 1 & 2. This person will lead a diverse workforce to focus on the mission and create a quality culture by providing employee input, motivation, rewards and reasonable security. In return, members of the organization are willing to pledge their loyalty.

Flow or Discord?

The impact of a manager's style can be summed up as either one of flow or discord. The same individual may use both, depending upon the situation, however, most will follow one or the other. Either the manager tries to remove barriers to keep the company moving smoothly towards its goals or the manager intervenes to re-direct people. The first is cooperative in nature, the latter is disruptive.

Generally, a manager who seeks the course of *flow* will, over time, achieve better cooperation and results from the people being directed. This is because this approach drives out fear and helps the organization concentrate on the customer. On the other hand, discord steers the focus back on the boss and re-directs energy to please him or her.

General Electric was one of the first companies to evaluate management style in regards to leaders getting along with subordinates or risk being unemployed. Honda rates its managers by how many associates they have been able to help since the last evaluation.

Most managers realize that there is little time available for the details that will help shape and develop the "best style." They have a wide range of responsibilities — from the training of subordinates to earning the mutual trust of fellow team members.

When a manager is working excessively long hours, it is time to step back and reflect on the following:

1. Am I spending too much time on details that should be delegated?
2. Is there a "trust issue" that needs to be resolved?

Three Vital Factors

The three elements that determine the success or failure of managers are style, performance, and the relationship with the person to whom they report.

Problems may be caused by:

- An approach to management that does not conform to the organization's culture.
- Performance that is not acceptable to those in power — even though the standard of what is acceptable may keep changing.

It is the "difference in style" that determines the level of comfort or discomfort on the part of those grading the performance. If results are negative and management style is "different," then style can be an assignable cause and a management change made to "solve the problem." However, if performance is decreasing and the management technique is the same, or comfortable to those doing the grading, the chances are much better that external causes will be blamed — and the feeling conveyed that everything possible is being done to improve performance.

As the following chart illustrates, several combinations of this relationship exist.

Relationship of Management Style and Performance

STYLE		PERFORMANCE	
	Same	less vulnerable	safe
	Different	vulnerable	safe for now
		Poor	Good

Difference in Management Style Makes the Difference

For maximum results we need to analyze the effectiveness of the executive style in relationship to solving current problems and providing long term leadership.

It is a fact of human nature that change, no matter

whether it is good or bad, will give improved results for awhile. The goal is to seek management that provides both short term and long term high performance.

Remember, management style and quality culture are inseparably linked. Be sure your methods support the mission.

6

Hail to the Chief!

The life of a Chief Executive Officer is often lonely. It resembles the refrain of an old song by "The Reverend Mister Black": "You must walk that lonesome valley, you must walk it by yourself. No one else can walk it for you; you must walk it by yourself."

After the discussions have ended and the recommendations have been offered, someone has to make the difficult decisions. This is the time when the education is over and the "execution" takes place.

The higher you climb the ladder the more demanding the job becomes. In an interview on the Larry King Show,

Vice President Al Gore stated that the President of the U.S. makes, on average, eight major decisions a day while a CEO may make two a week.

What does this signify? Complexity, with a capital C! As the volume and magnitude of the work increases the amount of time that can be devoted to each decision becomes less and less. That's why managers and CEOs can never be over-prepared. The next assignment may not leave time for learning — only *doing*.

The position of Chief Executive Officer in a company is the supreme paradox of power and pressure. The individual is entrusted with the power, in the form of authority, to lead the organization in whatever way he or she chooses. The results — how well the enterprise understands and performs — provides the pressure.

If the performance is excellent the CEO is highly rewarded as it is much easier to reward *one* instead of many. If the performance is poor the CEO is replaced since, by the same token, it is much easier to replace one instead of many.

This is not some hidden fact. It is known to every member of the organization.

What About the Stakeholders?

Every CEO "worth his salt" understands the need to provide a return to those who play a meaningful role in the project.

The major stakeholders usually include:

- Shareholders or partners — suppliers of equity.
- Customers — users of products or services.
- Suppliers — providers of goods or services to *make* products or services.
- Employees — suppliers of "human capital."
- Governmental agencies — that tax, regulate, and make laws that affect the organization's every move and long term strategies.
- Community — the "neighborhood" in which the organization is located; where the surrounding environment determines the quality of life for both employees and residents.
- Bankers — providers of debt.
- Board of Directors — suppliers of advice and approval.
- The analysts — concern and recommendations from Wall Street.
- Labor unions — may represent some of the employees.

When you survey this list you begin to understand the dilemma of the CEO. W*hat* return for *which* stakeholders?

It is extremely difficult to make good decisions that

will please all the parties equally. In fact, it is impossible. It is inevitable that at some point the chief executive officer will be in disfavor with some or all of the stakeholders, placing his or her job at risk.

The objective of both the organization and the CEO is the same: survival.

It is vital that the top executive continues to listen, communicate, and cooperate with *all* who have a vested interest. They have a right to expect this. If the CEO is not available to them, they will find someone else who is.

Each stakeholder has objectives for their contribution to the success of the organization. Their question, however, is "When will I receive my reward?"

Long term goals.

It is difficult for the CEO to sell the "big picture" because the vision is for the future, not the present. Issues that concern many of the constituents include:

- Borrowing money for growth without being strangled by too much debt.
- Putting time and money into employee training rather than larger salary increases.

- Taking time to build lasting partnerships with both customers and suppliers as opposed to seeking only immediate returns.

Short term goals.

After hearing people ask "What have you done for me lately?" many CEO's fall into a pattern of becoming nearsighted. They base every decision on how they can look good on the upcoming quarterly, semi-annual and annual report.

When this cycle becomes established, the performance is expected to be repeated without fail in every reporting period. This often leaves no room for expenditures for research and development or attention to needed capital expansion.

What will eventually transpire? The organization will soon be operating to fulfill only short term goals and the long term objectives will be swept aside.

If you don't plan for the future, there may be no future.

Culture and Credibility

Many top executives desire to put their trademark or "pawprint" on the company. And the manner in which this is done has a direct effect on the culture. In fact the employees look to the leader to find out what the "in" culture will be. However, every organization is steeped in tradition so the impact may only be superficial.

A larger issue is that many CEOs are suffering from a credibility gap. When the person in charge is able to command a substantial annual compensation package — while many in the organization are in jeopardy of either losing their jobs or being told to "do more with less" — there is an ethics question of fairness.

When good performance means the leader gets a "lot more" and the rest of the people get a "little more" the gap widens. Then, when the results of the company are poor and the top executive stays while others are told to leave, there is often bitterness.

Top Down, or Bottom Up?

The CEO, and the entire management team, must demonstrate leadership from the top down while employees must be empowered to participate from the bottom up. The ultimate goal is management that will have the facts, receive the cooperation, and demonstrate enthusiasm throughout the organization to carry out a single agenda. Management's task becomes one of developing the best plan possible and to keep the company focused and staying away from a constant fight over turf in a multi-agenda environment. Individuals must be able to center on the company's objectives instead of putting all their efforts on their own plans.

It is unfortunate when too much time is spent by executives in protecting turf, expanding power bases, and promoting self-interest — all of which is very evident to the manual and clerical employees.

This is why most workers are receptive to the changes brought about by a quality culture. They see and relate to the need for a new system.

Top leadership, however, fearful of a loss of power, may be against it. The next line of management has been taught to "please the boss" so they also echo alarm at such a change. They too are eager to gain power. Average employees only resist the transformation when their job security seems to be in jeopardy.

Often, the workers feel like the pig who was discussing the farmer's breakfast of ham and eggs with a chicken. The chicken was delighted, but the pig was really down in the dumps. When the chicken asked the pig what was wrong, he replied, "For you it is only a contribution but for me it is a total commitment!"

Workers sometimes feel they are the only ones who

are making a commitment. They would like to be sure everyone is.

The CEO, the executives, the managers, the supervisors and every employee must be unanimous and declare, "This is *our* company. *We are committed!* We are in this thing together!"

7

The Pressure to Perform

A primary reason given for changes in management or for people losing their jobs is "lack of performance." From every side we are constantly bombarded by the need for measurable outcomes and bottom line results.

This phenomena has been accompanied by CEO's receiving enormous compensation packages for "extraordinary" progress; or at least the promise of success.

The proper interpretation of financial data is critical in making the correct decisions. Significant changes on both the income statement and the balance sheet can come by acquisition, merger or divestiture. It usually takes several years before the true result of these moves are known. There will also be yearly swings in income due to the cyclical nature of the economy, weather, and world events which in combination are called the *business cycle.* How a company reacts to these changes is often more important than just looking at the numbers.

Unfortunately, in today's investor-driven market, a "down year" is rarely tolerated and top managers are often asked to resign. Instead of making decisions that will be best in the long run, these leaders often feel forced to make hasty short term decisions for the sake of survival.

The president of a Fortune 500 company had these words in needle point, framed and hanging on his office wall:

"Bad Numbers Will Get You Every Time."

Since the boom after World War II, the nation's economy has gone through swings of growth and stagnation, but always with an overall upward trend. Population increases have continued. Inflation has taken various swipes at eroding real growth, peaking during the Carter administration and into the early Reagan years. Then a period of deflation followed.

It has become normal for management, when questioned on performance, to look for scapegoats to fire and then move ahead. Of course incompetent people and poor performers need to be removed, but the style of many managers is to shuffle people in and out of the revolving door without getting to the root cause of the problems.

For many years our productivity and quality in the United States held off competition from abroad. Workers felt their jobs were secure and could count on employment if they worked hard and made the effort to succeed. It was believed that loyalty and commitment was a two way street and that employees were to be protected as "family."

Today, that relationship has been badly shaken.

- Private companies have become "public" and investors pressure for results that are often impossible.
- The "rate of return" has become the motto of both the providers of capital and the Board of Directors
- Competition is now world wide in nature, often favoring plants in other countries.

The Load of Leverage

Because normal business swings did not produce the type of investor excitement that Wall Street desired, a new way to create wealth was invented. In the 1980s we discovered how to build a fortune out of "air." It's called the *leveraged buyout.*

Here's how it operates. A group of investors assembles a large block of cash or credit and will "cozy up" to the CEO of a company with the promise of extreme wealth if he or she will play ball. A plan is formulated and shareholders are offered a price per share that is substantially above the current market price for the stock. The shareholders are bought out, the company taken private — and laden with a tremendous burden of debt.

At this point the spider (the investors) has trapped the fly (the CEO). The new debt that is suddenly piled on the company must be satisfied and it becomes not only the daily burden but the total agenda.

How is the debt load paid? In most cases it is by the termination of employees through various schemes. Often the firings are not based on good or bad performance, or even whether or not they were needed. The layoffs are strictly a matter of cutting costs sufficiently to handle the interest payments on the debt.

What about the survivors? They are faced with an overload of work, and often the guilt of surviving. Those remaining are usually those who can do the work, but are paid the least. As one CEO put it, "Our only hope is that advanced technology can replace the valuable experience we have lost."

By the Numbers

The universal measuring stick for managers is the budget. The exercise usually takes place about six months prior to the beginning of a new year and has been called "Hell week for managers."

In late fall, after a great deal of arguing over numbers — past and present — the budget is completed.

Often the process is one of gamesmanship between the corporate office (where the top management and the accountants reside) and the field (where much of the money is spent).

It may be well into the first quarter of the new year before the Board of Directors approves the budget since they may want to know the final results of the previous year. At that point the numbers are etched in stone as an absolute measuring stick.

Regardless of the dynamics that are impacting the organization the CEO is expected to meet the budget. If performance is less than what was planned it is considered unsatisfactory. If it exceeds the forecast you were "sand-bagging." Only by staying right on course with the budget are you judged to "manage well."

Leadership cannot and should not be able to walk away from accountability, but a system that rewards managing change is equally important as one that rewards managing the budget.

J. Douglas Brown of Princeton University, after 50 years of observation, stated: "Perhaps the simplest way to point up the difference between a leadership-centered and a control-centered management of human organization is to remind ourselves that dollars can be budgeted but human motivation can't."[1]

Brown observed that as a frame of reference in respect to funds available, budgets are essential. But "as a device for developing greater leadership, enthusiasm, dedication, reliability, cooperation, or for building the organization and improving its quality, budgets are a dull reflection of the machines used in their elaboration."

What about Rewards?

We know that performance improves through cooperation, yet when it comes to compensation we seem to operate in a dense fog.

Managers have "perfected" a system of individual pay ranges, individual goals, and individual performance analysis to the point that we don't know how to change it. As one executive recently told me, "I'm ready to trash our pay system and start over!"

The phrase "What gets rewarded gets done," is true. However, in our collective wisdom we have decided that every individual has different talents and that each of these contributions is worth a different amount, even though they may spend equal time at the task.

The disparity in earnings is based on a series of judgments usually made by management and approved by the Board of Directors. When unions become involved, there may be a contract that allows negotiations on compensation and the length and terms of the contract.

In his book, *The Democratic Corporation*, Russell A. Ackoff, explains that "A uniform, explicit, and operationally unambiguous measure of performance that incorporates some function of the amount of profit generated — for example, return on capital employed — can be applied to units at every level, including the executive office. This makes possible comparison of the performances of units at all levels and discourages 'make work' and bureaucracy."[2]

What Happened to the Golden Rule?

Headlines in recent years have told of plant closings and massive layoffs to reduce costs. In many instances this may be the only prudent course of action for the entire company to remain healthy — much like the cutting of the diseased branch of a tree. But when this is done without logic or reason the respect, loyalty, and commitment of the workforce is lost almost immediately.

No one is saying that business catastrophes can be completely avoided, but here is what is increasingly clear:

The health of an organization is greatly improved when workers are viewed as equals in the management-employee relationship.

The connectivity of performance, security and compensation form the very heart of a quality culture and these issues must be addressed. It requires a participative management approach where the overall mission of the company becomes the agenda for everyone involved.

For too long employees have come to the conclusion that the Golden Rule of management is "I have the gold and I make the rules." Managers who are committed to introducing a quality culture must operate by the *real* Golden Rule: "Do unto others as you would have others do unto you."

It is against this backdrop that the element of performance must be viewed. Each participant must be measured and rewarded in a manner that is accepted as equitable by all for a true quality culture to succeed.

In the Zone

There is a direct correlation between team efforts and improved performance.

In our book *The Culture of Success*, we introduced the concept of the Zone of Improvement.

The Zone of Improvement

As Applied to Improving Employee Contribution

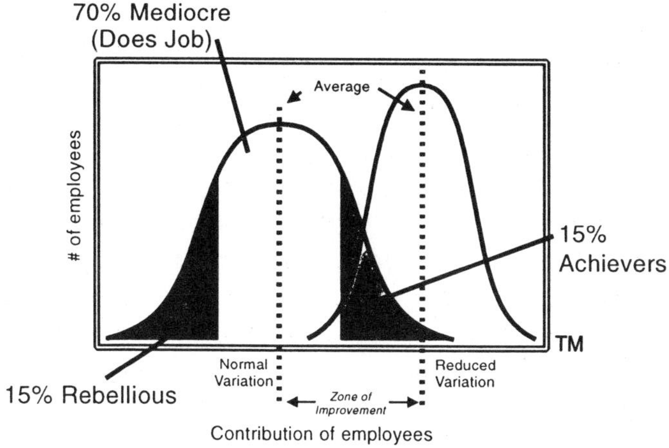

If a task, or learning effort is easy, the bell curve — the distribution — will spread (wide variation in the performance of people) and tend to move to the left — toward the direction of poor performance.

On the other hand, if the requirement is demanding and everyone feels accountable for the improvement of others, the curve will narrow (shrinking the variation in the performance of people) and move to the right — toward the direction of improvement.

By cultivating a working environment of cooperation to replace a culture of internal competition we can drive out fear and reduce the human variation in the work place. When everyone starts helping each other to improve, the "best" get better and the low performers actually become as proficient as the former highest performers.

Of course, there will always be a few who choose mediocrity. A manager then has a decision to make: either let them stay knowing that they will not improve or show them the door.

Jack Welch, CEO of General Electric, observes: "One thing I've learned is the value of stretching the organization, by setting the bar higher than people think they can go. The standard of performance we use is: be as good as the best in the world. Invariably people find the way to get there, or most of the way. They dream and reach and search. The trick is not to punish those who fall short. If they improve, you reward them - even if they haven't reached the goal. But unless you set the bar high enough, you'll never find out what people can do."[3]

Today, "performance" has become too important to leave to executives alone. Organizations that will survive are those that share everything from budgeting to bottom line results with every employee — involving people at all levels in the planning and decision process.

Managing for results means more than a profitable income statement and a healthy balance sheet. It involves *people* — their collective efforts, their collective results, and their collective rewards. At the same time, the burden of both accountability and responsibility rests heavily on the leadership. This is the challenge of management and is what differentiates it from the "rest of the work."

8

The Interactive Partnership

Every organization, whether it be a church, a school, a business, or whatever, has a product or service it makes available to the market — to the customer. How well the organization accomplishes this depends on the *interactivity component* of the management system.

What is interactivity? It is the communication, cooperation, conflict resolution, and approach to competition which are all closely aligned with *culture*.

Culture is the *background*, interactivity is the *foreground*, and the management style is the *link*.

The ingredients we are discussing provide the win-win opportunities that make it possible to move an organization to the highest possible level.

In the past, negotiations between customer and supplier have usually resulted in a win-lose situation. That doesn't have to be the case. It can be replaced by "partnering" — a culture of cooperation where the needs of both are mutually satisfied. The same approach can be used in labor relations to work out agreements with the bargaining unit. It can also be used as a collaborative in the governmental regulatory process.

Communication and cooperation have different meaning to different people and their effectiveness is often difficult to measure.

There is a tool, however, that has proven very effective in implementing this process. It is called Quality Functional Deployment.[1] QFD has been described as "a planning methodology that ensures that the voice of the customer is understood, prioritized, documented, and integrated into your company's actions."[2]

The Agreement

Before such a process can be used successfully a partnership *agreement* between customer and supplier must be worked out. To be effective, representatives from participating enterprises need to move toward a written document signed by the CEO's of both companies.

To emphasize the mutual sincerity, a series of commitments should be drawn up. This document should:

- Create a shared vision.
- Formalize the communication process.
    - Schedule frequent visits.
    - Develop an evaluation process.
- Establish (together) "best performance practices."
- Jointly develop the planning process in terms of product development, testing, production dates, and delivery schedules.
- Reduce costs in a win-win relationship.
- Empower both work forces to participate in the planning process.
- Encourage a learning relationship for the purpose of continual improvement.
- Mutually develop "value added" for the benefit of both partners.

The document should be worked out by cross-functional teams from each company. The duties of the teams should be defined. This will form the basis for an ongoing, mutually beneficial partnership.

The Application

Let's look at a unique application of QFD to show

how it can be integrated with the management system to listen to the voice of all of the primary stakeholders of an organization.

In Chapter 6 we discussed the role of the primary stakeholders — customers, stockholders, suppliers, debt holders, governmental agencies and the community.

In return for their involvement, what do the stakeholders want from the organization?

- Return on investment of money or time (payment).
- Value and quality in terms of products, services and relationships.
- Knowledge of the future direction of the company and how it will impact them.
- Timely and accurate information.
- Compliance with laws, codes and regulations.
- A commitment and demonstration of high values and integrity (they must "walk the talk").
- The desire to be partners.

How is the management system going to deliver these ingredients?

Each component of the system contributes to these *wants* of the stakeholders. *How* the organization does this defines the structure and the performance targets that will be evaluated.

The Approach

To begin the QFD approach, a *reference point* of where we are now must be established for each of the six inter-related components (Leadership, Power, Culture, Accountability, Interactivity and Responsibility).

Next, we apply what is known as the "Pugh Concept Selection Process" — a unique method of choosing the best alternative that was developed by Stewart Pugh of Great Britain. It is a simple, effective technique worth considering.

In this case we will compare the *criteria* (what the stakeholders are seeking) with the *concept* (what we now have).

The current leadership style needs to be reviewed to see if it will deliver the results the stakeholders desire.

Here's an example.

In the following Pugh chart, the component of *leadership* is examined. The analysis is based on the premise that as organizational needs change, leadership styles must also change. The styles are compared against six different organizational needs.

Modified Pugh Concept Selection Chart

What Leadership Approach is Best
— Depending Upon the Organization's Need?

Leadership Approach						
NEED ▼	Strategic	Human Assets	Expertise	Control & Command	Change Master	Charisma
Direction	+3	+1	+1	+1	+1	+1
Empowerment	-1	+3	-1	-1	+1	-1
Identity	+1	+1	+3	+1	-1	-1
Control	+1	-1	+1	+3	-1	-1
Turn-around	+1	+1	-1	-1	+3	+1
Miracle	-1	+1	-1	-1	+1	+3
Total	+4	+6	+2	+2	+4	+2

Rating System: Excellent match = +3, Good = +1, Poor = -1

Define the current organization need, shown in the left hand column. Review the leadership approaches that can be taken.[3] Analyze which avenue is best for the current problem (shown in the example as +3), as well as, what might be the best overall strategy for the long term.

In this example, the Human Assets approach (which is the most common leadership style) rates as the best, followed by Strategic and Change Master. Strategic is favored when the direction is the most important need.

Change Master approach is utilized when a turnaround is required.

By taking each of our six components through a matrix, we can determine what we want to keep and what we must change in our current management system. This process can help tell us what kind of organization we should become, how we will be structured, and what we will measure.

One of the great benefits of evaluating various alternatives is that the process generates new alternatives.

There has been endless discussion on the concepts of "Cooperation through partnering," "Rebuilding a management system to deliver what the stakeholders want," and "Incorporating an evaluation approach for accountability."

Now, through the use of these dynamic interactivity techniques, these processes can come alive.

9

Who is Responsible?

A newly appointed manager was being indoctrinated into a reengineering program. After listening for awhile, she thought, "This sounds like something we tried once before. Why can't our top management just sit down and decide what they want to do, let us know what it is, and leave well enough alone?"

In many organizations, employees see management introducing programs and problem solving techniques in a predictable pattern: hype about the program, introduction, training, and then very little follow through. Soon another new program is introduced and the previous one is forgotten. Supervisors and employees learn: "If you ignore it, it will go away."

A more long term version is the "pendulum approach," which is used to radically change the structure. An example is going from a centralized organization to decentralized then back again. First centralizing for control, then decentralizing for autonomy — always hoping the change will produce better results.

Although every organization is constantly evolving, there are certain responsibilities leaders must assume that will provide stability and direction.

There are No "They's"

A common misconception of managers is that if they do a good job, someone "higher up" will give them their next assignment. That's not the way it works.

In most cases, the responsibility for growth, development and change in a designated area is up to the person who has been placed in charge. He or she is accountable for the planning, the process and the performance that will make the future better than the past. No one has a secret plan hidden away to tell you what to do. The burden rests squarely on your shoulders.

Designing a blueprint for the future is a key part of your assignment, but it cannot be done in a vacuum. It must fit into the strategic plan for the entire organization. Yet no one else is going to decipher how your piece of the puzzle fits. That is your job — to work with your team and devise a plan.

Each manager must determine exactly what his job is, what skills are needed, which tools to use in which situations, and be constantly open to learning new techniques.

Despite our fascination with methods and systems, most of what we accomplish is done through people.

It is the responsibility of management to make optimal use of human assets.

Learn the Economics

Every business (or business segment) has a set of *numbers.* The economics we are talking about, however, are not found on a computer spreadsheet. Although industry statistics may be available and will provide a guide, they are only the starting point for decisions that are unique to your organization.

You may feel this analysis must be left to the accountants or financial officers, but your understanding is vital.

First, clearly define your business. By reviewing your own past financial records and those of your competitors during the past five to ten years, you should be able to determine how the organization is doing.

Second, compare your data with that of the industry. This will help you measure who spends what percentage of the sales dollar on material, labor, etc. Your first inclination may be, "Everyone does this, so what is the big deal!"

I think you will discover that everyone does *not* undertake this analysis.

By repeating this exercise on an on-going basis, you will be able to develop the economics in a way that expected returns can be predicted — based on the industry, your company's abilities, and the marketplace.

You'll begin to understand that how much money remains after you sell a product or service depends on (1) the price the market will bear and (2) the cost to your company to provide it.

You will also learn that the narrower your market niche, the less price competition — and the lower your cost versus competition, the better chance you have at higher margins.

To make the best decisions requires both an understanding of the managing process and the need for cross-functional representation from all the systems in a company. Remember that marketing, financial, manufacturing, and engineering decisions cannot be made separately. They are all inter-related.

Core Competencies

There are particular skill areas in which every manager should seek training, investigation, and experience. They include:

- Employee (labor) relations.
- Training.
- Improving productivity (process and product knowledge).
- Cost control (knowing what to measure).
- Quality control (meeting customer expectations).
- Inventory control (learning to do more, with less).
- Market analysis.
- Purchasing (supplier relationships).
- Decision making.
- Problem solving.
- Conflict resolution.
- Business law.
- Strategic planning.

In addition, there should be financial training that includes:

- Cash flow reports.
- Income statement.
- Balance sheet.

- Variation analysis.
- Budgeting.
- Proformas/forecasting.
- Auditing.

In my experience, the best way to have managers accept accountability based on the information in the "monthly figures" is to meet as a group and look at the results of charting the variables. An outside service takes the monthly financial data and charts it against targets and previous years results. The owner of the chart — the manager involved — then has the opportunity to comment and to seek cooperation from his peers to solve problems related to that variable.

The outside company supplies not only the charts, but a facilitator. This takes the internal personalities out of the equation and focuses on resolving the issues. The process is extremely effective.

Developing an Operating Philosophy

In my early years as a manager at Brockway Glass, the two mentors I mentioned in Chapter 1 (my father, Richard A. Jacobs and Lewis F. Gayner) taught me the necessity of developing an operating philosophy. It not only must be adopted by the company, but espoused by every corporate leader.

Here is how the philosophy was stated at Brockway:

1. To create and maintain the highest morale for all employees.
2. To be the best managed company in our industry.
3. To be the most respected company in our industry by our customers, our employees, and in our communities.
4. To maintain the highest possible profit potential.
5. To be committed to being a growth company.

This outlook was "actualized" by the following concepts of operation:

1. The sales department will utilize and conform to production equipment.
2. Production support services will provide liaison with sales.
3. Processes will be standardized to control or eliminate variables and to develop people more quickly. (Remember, standards are dynamic, not static and that this is a team effort, no attempt to develop experts.)
4. Conservative accounting principles will be used.
5. We will maintain uniform personnel policies.

What were the results of placing the philosophy and

operating concepts into practice at Brockway Inc.?

1. Complete interchangeability of equipment in thirteen plants located throughout the United States and also applicable in many other countries via technical service agreements. (This interchangeability of equipment was unknown at that time in the industry.)
2. Superior quality — industry leader.
3. Lower costs — industry leader.
4. All thirteen glass container plants contributed and focused on "the company" even though they were competing with each other. The reward was for total company success.
5. Highest productivity in industry measured monthly by an independent agency for all plants in the United States.

After seventeen years of learning these concepts at Brockway Glass Company, I was given the opportunity to lead a management team at Brockway Plastics Company. The utilization of these same concepts turned a small division into an industry leader, moving from the loss column to a profitable company in the first year.

Who is "Number One?"

What I learned at Brockway and in the leadership assignments which have followed is that the greatest responsibility of the manager is to recognize that the customer always comes first. Without satisfied users of its products or services the best performing company on the planet will not survive. This is true of schools, hospitals, churches, businesses, and industries. The only exceptions are some government programs, foundations and endowed organizations.

Equally important is to recognize that it is futile to play the "blame game" or attempt to divert accountability for your actions. In the words of an old proverb: "To whom much is given, much is required."

Who is responsible? As a manager, the answer is *you!*

10

Where Do We Go From Here?

More than four decades ago Peter Drucker called management "A study of the most important function in American society."[1]

His words still remain true, but what about the future? I believe the tremendous technological advances we are experiencing make "good managing" a commodity whose value is increasing. The openness of our culture, the advent of a world market with global transportation and communication systems, plus the complex nature of people coming into the work place, all point toward the premium that good management can and should command.

Dealing with people in today's society is difficult

enough, but keeping them motivated to learn and achieve at an ever-accelerating pace is truly a challenge.

People continue to ask: "What training, guidance, or example can we give to prepare individuals to assume and succeed in positions of future leadership?" "Where will the managers of tomorrow be developed?"

Let's be honest. We must acknowledge the erosion of our public education system and realize that many students are not prepared for college. Yet at the same time we see our graduate schools packed — often with students from other cultures where the work ethic and the value of education are still highly embraced.

It's time to return to basics.

Certain fundamental educational skills need to be taught and learned. Essential social skills must be re-discovered.

In a world that is overwhelmed by an avalanche of data, how can people with limited educational skills and practically no experience in either the individual or group dynamics of "work" possibly know what to do with the flood of facts and figures coming their way?

Does History Repeat?

Since the close of World War II when many of the war time applications to problem solving were adopted by organizations, we have seen a continuous stream of "miracle cures" offered to businesses. However, it only takes a casual observation to realize that problems still remain.

History *does* repeat itself. We see certain management approaches tried, discarded, and later reinvented and renamed. What is the basic and reoccurring phenomena that all this activity is trying solve?

Steps on the Journey

The objectives we are attempting to reach are found in what I call "The Eleven Step Journey to Enlightened Management."

Step 1: Persuade people to cooperate and work together without undue conflict to achieve positive results.

Step 2: Motivate everyone in the organization to surpass the competition.

Step 3: Encourage and train all workers to utilize the resources of the organization to the greatest benefit of all its stakeholders.

Step 4: Stress the importance of the customer and his or her complete satisfaction with the products or services so that a continued partnership can and *will* develop.

Step 5: Prepare people within the organization to continue the work after those currently in authority move on.

Step 6: Abide by the established principles and ethics to become and remain a good corporate citizen of the community and a law abiding asset to the nation.

Step 7: Incorporate a review and planning process to make sure the organization is on course and the mission remains relevant and achievable. If not, make the necessary adjustments.

Step 8: Review all decisions so that positive ones will be duplicated and the negative will be viewed as experiences that won't be repeated.

Step 9: Treat people with dignity and respect. Recognize their efforts.

Step 10: Make sure that all members of the organization enjoy what they do. If not, find out why and correct it.

Step 11: Learn to address and deal with difficult situations in a manner that speaks well of the organization and its people. If unpopular actions must be taken, administer them fairly and professionally.

Managing Change

In recent years numerous techniques have been developed to help make these steps steady and firm. The shelves of bookstores and libraries are filled with solutions addressing one or more of these issues.

Why do we still not know all the answers? Perhaps Thomas Jefferson described it best when he wrote in the preamble to the Declaration of Independence, "When in the course of human events . . ."

Herein lies the problem.

The relationships between and among people are in constant change — producing an endless cycle of conflicts to be addressed and resolved.

This also describes the daily duties of an active, "involved" manager.

The manager who hides, hoping the difficulties will somehow disappear is only compounding the problem.

You only need to thumb through the books addressing these questions to understand that management is not defined by a single issue. It is a process comprised of interrelated components which are acting either in harmony or discord with each other.

The "technique" manuals are intended to solve a particular facet of the puzzle. Only by taking an in-depth look at each of these proficiencies do we begin to understand the immense size of the tool kit available to managers.

In the final analysis, choosing the right tools for the right task is up to you.

You're the Coach

I believe the same three factors that produce a winning football team will bring success in management.

> *Confidence:* from the leadership (coaching).
> *Motivation:* the emotion to achieve and win.
> *Recruiting and training:* building a team of people with skills and abilities.

In a traditional culture, management controls, commands, and directs. In a quality culture, management communicates, cooperates, and coaches. Leadership retains its responsibility for performance, but it becomes a *shared* responsibility with an empowered workforce that joins in the decision process and actively participates in problem resolution and the reward system.

The ultimate triumph of an organization rests not only with our ability to understand technology, but with our continued desire to understand each other.

Throughout history, regardless of the geography, the economic climate or the severity of the problem, it is the *people* part of the puzzle that ultimately solves the dilemma.

For that reason managers must be keenly aware of the signals they are sending. If we post signs that read "People are Our Most Important Asset," we can't treat them as a commodity with an unlimited supply.

"I Will!"

The concepts we have presented must become more than fascinating ideas or thoughts to consider for the future. Leadership is needed now.

Here are personal commitments you can make regarding the six inter-related components of management.

1. I will provide **leadership** by giving vision, values, direction, strategy and encouragement.
2. I will not misuse the **power** I have been given.
3. I will seek to make the **culture** of the organization a *quality* culture.
4. I will accept **accountability** by measuring performance and being answerable for the bottom line.
5. I will promote **interactivity** both inside and outside my organization.
6. I will assume **responsibility** for accepting tasks, taking risks, solving problems, making decisions and completing the work.

It is my desire that your commitment will become part of a philosophy, an attitude, an approach and a system that will make a positive impact on your organization and on the lives you touch. These are the true rewards of *managing for success*.

References

CHAPTER ONE

1. A. H. Maslow, *Motivation and Personality*, New York: Harper & Brothers Publishers, 1954, p. 39.
2. Ron Read, "The Engineer in Transition to Management," *Industrial Engineering Solutions*, September, 1996, p.23.
3. Douglas McGregor, *Leadership and Motivation,* Cambridge, MA: M.I.T. Press, 1966, p.13.

CHAPTER TWO

1. Peter M. Senge, *The Fifth Discipline Fieldbook,* New York: Doubleday, 1994, p. 89.
2. Russell L. Ackoff, *The Democratic Corporation,* New York: Oxford University Press, 1994, p.20.
3. Peter V. Vaill, *Learning as a Way of Being*, San Francisco: Jossey-Bass Inc., Publishers, 1996, p.109.

CHAPTER THREE

1. Tsun-Yan Hsieh, "Leadership Actions," *The McKinsey Quarterly*, 1990 (4th Quarter), pp. 43-45.
2. Jack Welch, quoted in Noel M. Tichy and Stratford Sherman, *Control Your Destiny or Someone Elise Will*, New York: Harper Business Press, 1994, p.195.
3. Warren Bennis and Burn Nanus, *Leaders: The Strategies for Taking Charge,* New York: Harper & Row, 1985, p.7.

CHAPTER FOUR

1. John P. Kotter, *Power in Management*, New York: AMACON Publications, 1979, p. 81.

2. John Dew, "Creating Team Leaders," *Journal for Quality and Participation,* October-November, 1995, p. 53.

CHAPTER FIVE

1. Neil H, Snyder, James J. Dowd, Jr., and Dianne M. Houghton, *Vision, Values and Courage: Leadership for Quality Management,* New York: The Free Press (Macmillan), 1994, p. 26.

CHAPTER SEVEN

1. J. Douglas Brown, *The Human Nature of Organizations*, New York: AMACON, 1973, p. 48.
2. Russell L. Ackoff, *The Democratic Corporation,* New York: Oxford University Press, 1994, p. 195.
3. Jack Welch, quoted in Noel Tichy and Stratford Sherman, *Control Your Destiny of Someone Else Will*, New York: Harper Business Press, 1994, p. 300.

CHAPTER EIGHT

1. QFD is a licensed product of the American Suppler Institute, Allen Park, Michigan. ASI is a nonprofit corporation dedicated to improving the competitive position of U.S. industry.

NOTE: Quality function deployment (QFD) is a planning tool brought to this country from Japan and developed into a line of products by ASI. QFD encourages cross-functional teamwork to help identify, understand, document and integrate customer requirements into a company's products and services.

2. *Quality Function Deployment Workshop Manual* (Version 5.4), Allen Park, MI, American Supplier Institute, 1995, pp. 6-30,31.
3. John C. Maxwell, *Learning Different Leadership Approaches,* Vol. 12, No. 3 series of Injoy Life Club, San Diego: Injoy Publishing, 1996, pp.1-6.

CHAPTER TEN

1. Peter Drucker, *The Practice of Management,* New York: Harper & Row Publishers, 1954.

About the Authors

Richard A. Jacobs, P.E. earned his undergraduate degree in industrial engineering at The Pennsylvania State University and his master's degree at Lehigh University where he also taught. Starting as a summer laborer, his industrial experience covers a number of management assignments with Brockway Inc., including manager of a glass plant and president of a plastics subsidiary. He was president and CEO of National Gas & Oil, Co, Inc., and now serves as a manager for Columbia Gas of Ohio. In addition to his current corporate activities, Jacobs is an author, speaker, seminar leader and consultant in the areas of management, quality culture, and organizational change. He is a registered Professional Engineer (P.E.). Jacobs is co-author of *The Culture of Success.*

Charles B. Dygert, Ph. D. began his career as a tool and die maker for General Motors. He earned his Bachelors, Masters and Doctorate degrees from Ohio State University and served on their faculty for 19 years. Dygert served with the industrial-development team that brought Honda of America to Ohio. He was awarded the coveted CPAE (Council of Peers Award for Excellence), a designation of the National Speakers Association. As a distinguished speaker on leadership, motivation, productivity and team building, he has given over 2500 presentations in all 50 states and in several foreign countries during the past twenty-five years. Dygert is author of *Success is a Team Effort* and co-author of *The Culture of Success.*

To schedule the authors for seminars, conventions or corporate training, contact:

Richard A. Jacobs
1705 Dry Creek Road
Granville, OH 43023

PHONE: (614) 587-3712
FAX: 1-614-392-4357

Dr. Charles B. Dygert
Motivational Enterprises, Inc.
P.O. Box 28124
Columbus, OH 43228

PHONE: 1-800-729-1293
FAX: 1-614- 870-3136